IT'S TIME TO EAT CLAM CHOWDER

It's Time to Eat CLAM CHOWDER

Walter the Educator

Silent King Books
A WhichHead Entertainment Imprint

Copyright © 2024 by Walter the Educator

All rights reserved. No part of this book may be reproduced in any manner whatsoever without written per- mission except in the case of brief quotations embodied in critical articles and reviews.

First Printing, 2024

Disclaimer

This book is a literary work; the story is not about specific persons, locations, situations, and/or circumstances unless mentioned in a historical context. Any resemblance to real persons, locations, situations, and/or circumstances is coincidental. This book is for entertainment and informational purposes only. The author and publisher offer this information without warranties expressed or implied. No matter the grounds, neither the author nor the publisher will be accountable for any losses, injuries, or other damages caused by the reader's use of this book. The use of this book acknowledges an understanding and acceptance of this disclaimer.

It's Time to Eat CLAM CHOWDER is a collectible early learning book by Walter the Educator suitable for all ages belonging to Walter the Educator's Time to Eat Book Series. Collect more books at WaltertheEducator.com

USE THE EXTRA SPACE TO TAKE NOTES AND DOCUMENT YOUR MEMORIES

CLAM CHOWDER

The clock strikes noon, it's time to eat,

It's Time to Eat Clam Chowder

A bowl of warmth, a special treat.

Clam chowder's ready, creamy and white,

Let's grab our spoons and take a bite!

The steam rises high, a cozy swirl,

Potatoes soft, give it a whirl.

Clams from the sea, so fresh, so sweet,

All in a bowl, it's quite the feat!

Dip in your bread, make it a boat,

Scoop up the soup, and let it float.

A sprinkle of herbs, a dash of care,

Each bite a hug that we can share.

"Mmm," says Mom, "It's nice and hot!"

"Don't eat too fast, or you'll burn your spot."

Blow on your spoon, take it slow,

The joys of chowder start to grow.

It's Time to Eat
Clam
Chowder

The flavors dance, so rich, so fine,

Clams, cream, and butter combine.

Potatoes and onions join the crew,

Every sip feels fresh and new.

"What's in the soup?" asks little Ben,

"It tastes like the ocean, again and again!"

The sea's salty waves, the wind's cool air,

A taste of adventure is hiding there!

Grandma adds crackers, one, two, three,

Crunchy companions, as happy as can be.

With every crumble, the flavors unite,

A perfect pair, it feels just right.

"Can I have seconds?" the kids all cheer,

Clam chowder's magic brings us near.

It warms our bellies, fills us with cheer,

It's Time to Eat
Clam Chowder

A meal so simple, yet so dear.

Outside, the wind begins to blow,

But inside, it's cozy, as we all know.

Around the table, we laugh and play,

Clam chowder brightens up our day.

So when it's cold or you need a treat,

Remember the joy of chowder to eat.

With clams and cream, it's truly divine,

It's Time to Eat
Clam Chowder

Time for clam chowder, a family time!

ABOUT THE CREATOR

Walter the Educator is one of the pseudonyms for Walter Anderson. Formally educated in Chemistry, Business, and Education, he is an educator, an author, a diverse entrepreneur, and he is the son of a disabled war veteran. "Walter the Educator" shares his time between educating and creating. He holds interests and owns several creative projects that entertain, enlighten, enhance, and educate, hoping to inspire and motivate you. Follow, find new works, and stay up to date with Walter the Educator™

at WaltertheEducator.com

www.ingramcontent.com/pod-product-compliance
Lightning Source LLC
LaVergne TN
LVHW052011060526
838201LV00059B/3970